© 2011 Disney

Which one is DIFFERENT?

1. He is a gloomy gray donkey.
2. What does Eeyore often lose?
3. ___ is the only character in the Hundred-Acre Wood who can fly.

WHO AM I?

Circle the correct answer.

Piglet   Pooh

tigger   Eeyore

Rabbit   Roo

© 2011 Disney

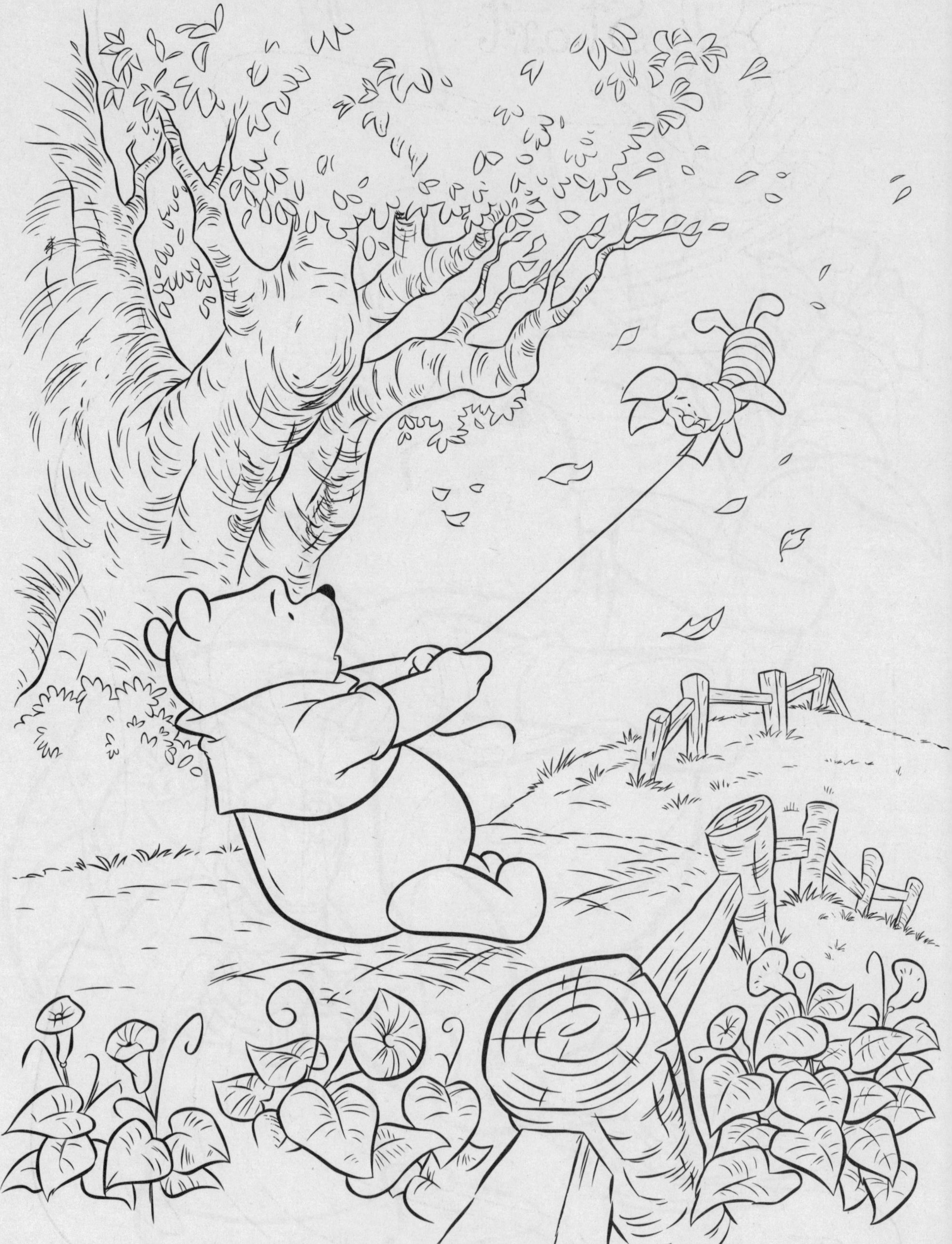

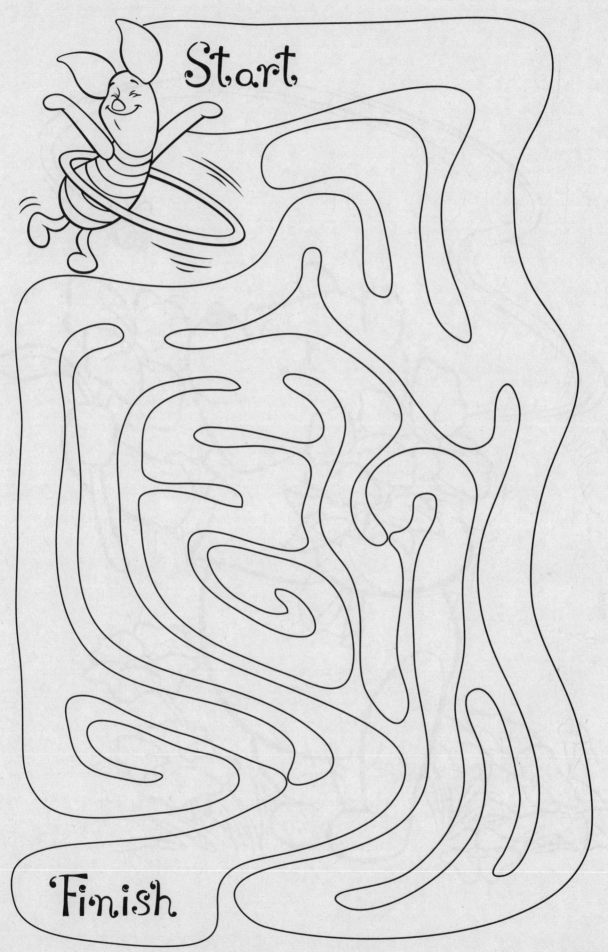

Start

Finish

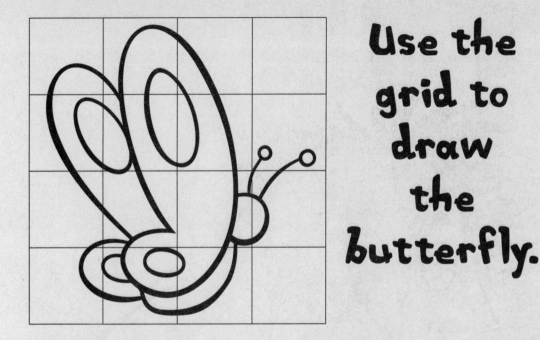

Use the grid to draw the butterfly.

© 2011 Disney

Look up, down, across, and diagonally for these words:

POOH	RABBIT
PIGLET	GOPHER
TIGGER	ROO
EEYORE	KANGA
OWL	BEES

```
S E E B T R R O O
I E O K E F N V W
B L E H A T P J R
S M P Y I N I X O
P O W B O C G Z W
G O B N T R L A L
Z A O M C B E H F
R Y U H K L L T T
G T I G G E R C P
```

Which line leads to Tigger?

ANSWER: A

Which one is DIFFERENT?

© 2011 Disney

Unscramble the names of these friends who live in the Hundred-Acre Wood.

ORO

_____

GRETGI

_____

OHPO

_____

BATIRB

_____

NAKGA

_____

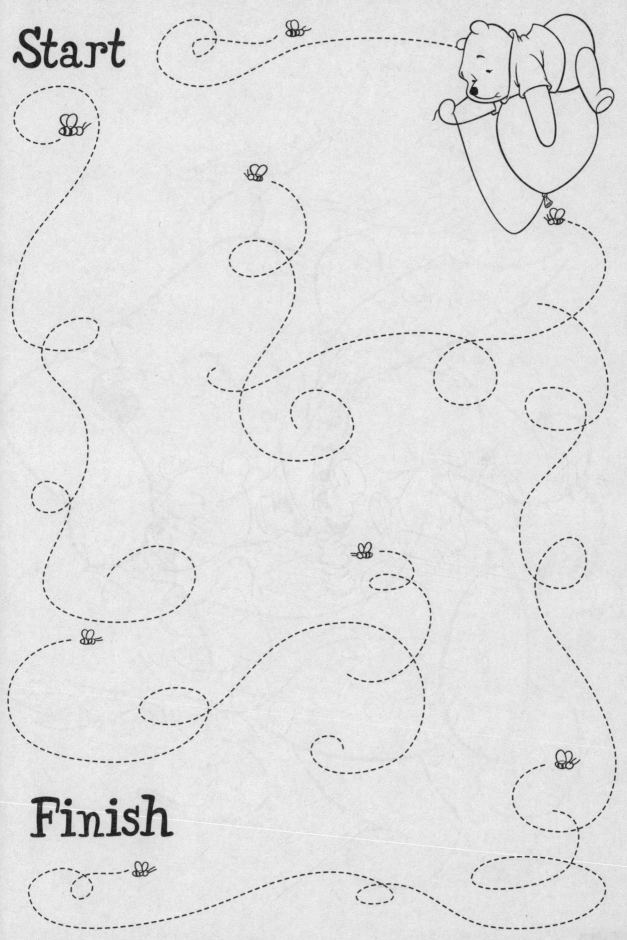

Start

Finish

WHO AM I?

Circle the correct answer.

Pooh   Piglet

Rabbit   tigger

Owl   Eeyore

Which line leads to Eeyore?

ANSWER: A